Coping With Grief

By Danette L. Simmons

Counseling Educational Materials

Introduction

Death is a very complicated part of life. All people, even adults struggle with death and grief. However, death and loss is part of our journey on earth.

Death happens to all living things, from blades of grass to frogs, dogs, and people.

The life of a fruit fly lasts just a day, but when it dies, this death is natural. The life of a tree, on the other hand, might last hundreds of years and this death is natural too. Death may seem hard and unfair, but everything that is alive right now will die someday and new things will be born or grow.

When we loose a pet, it is very hard and our heart may be filled with sadness. We can grieve for our lost pet, but in this coloring book were going to talk about how to cope with the loss of a person, a friend, or a family member.

What are some thoughts we can have when we first hear about the death of a person, a friend, or a family member?

❑ **FEAR THOUGHTS**
 Death is real and could happen to anyone. "I keep imaging how the person died."

❑ **WORRIED THOUGHTS**
"I am worried it could happen to my family member or another family member, or myself."

❑ **CONFUSED THOUGHTS**
"How can someone be alive one day and gone the next day?"

❑ **GUILT THOUGHTS**
If only I knew, I would have...

"I wish I would of spent more time with my loved one. I would have been more nice to that person if I only knew that they were going to die."

* It's normal to have these type of thoughts after a death. Talk with someone about your thoughts and feelings.

Where does a person go after they die?

No one really knows this answer. Many people have their own beliefs and have different answers, but many times it depends on our culture or religion.

Some people believe it means the end of life, but for many people, they believe it means our souls go to a new eternal life or afterlife in heaven. And it is there, that we will meet our loved ones again. Some people believe heaven is a very calm, peaceful, and beautiful place.

GRIEF

What is grief? Grief is a response to a loss of a loved one, whether it be a friend, family, or other close companion.

Grief can be an intense rolling waves of emotions for example, sad, shocked, frustrated, angry, frightened, confused, guilty, depressed, hopeful, and lonely. Sadness is a big part of grief.

When we lose a loved one, we may feel like crying a lot of the time, and we may feel so overwhelmed with sadness that we do not know how to cope with the loss of our loved one.

* It's normal to wish and hope that a loved one will come back to life.

STAGES OF GRIEF

Denial
(This isn't
happening to me!)

Anger (Why is this
happening to *me*?)

Depression (I don't *care*
anymore!)

Bargaining (I promise I'll be a
better person *if...*)

Acceptance (I still have to live
my life and have a purpose.

Color or draw how you're feeling or coping with grief.

Feeling

Death sometimes makes us feel uncomfortable and we don't know what to say to the person who lost a loved one.

Why?

We are afraid.

We are confused.

We don't understand how it could of happened.

*It's normal to have these feelings and thoughts.

How can I help
someone that is
experiencing a loss
of a loved one?

* Remember some people grieve for a couple of months to years, so be patient.

You can give gifts, food, flowers, a card, or letter.

* Never spread rumors or participate in them about the death of a person's loved one because it can hurt that person even more.

Keep something sentimental from that person for example, cards, pictures, letters, or painting.

How to Cope with Grief

Try to focus on the person's life and memories instead of the actual incident of death.

Talk to people you trust and can lean on. And as time goes by, we learn to come to the stage of acceptance, but that doesn't ever mean that we forget our loved one, but instead we are grateful for the memory and experience. We never forget them or love them any less.

When you talk about your feelings, you can then start the healing process. Here are some people you can consider talking to:

❏ FAMILY

If someone you love has died, chances are that your family members are going through many of the same emotions you are. It can help to talk to them about your memories and feelings, and to remind each other that you're all experiencing this together.

❏ TALK IT OUT WITH SOMEONE YOU TRUST

A grandpa, uncle, grandma, or aunt are a few examples. One of the best ways to let out your emotions, is to simply talk about them. There may be times when you feel like being alone with your thoughts, but talking to people you can rely on and trust can be a big help!

❏ A RELIGIOUS LEADER

It can be helpful to talk to your priest, pastor, rabbi, or other religious leader. These men and women have talked to many people who are dealing with death, and can counsel you on the process of grieving.

Grieving is a time when most people think a lot about faith, spirituality, and the afterlife, a religious leader can also help you sort through your feelings and beliefs on these subjects.

❏ A COUNSELOR

These are professionals who are trained to help you talk through whatever you're feeling or thinking about.

In a therapist's office, you can feel free to say whatever you want, and he or she must keep it confidential. * Some circumstances in regards to confidentiality may not apply if a person is not safe.

❑ TALK WITH OTHER KIDS THAT ARE DEALING WITH GRIEF.

Many organizations and groups hold special meetings where young people can get together to share thoughts and ideas, participate in activities, or just spend time together.

This is called "group counseling" or "group," and it can be very helpful. By meeting other kids who are going through almost the same thing, you will feel like you're not alone in your grief.

❑ CREATE AWARENESS:
Some people' find a purpose for their loved ones death, especially if there was an injustice or could have been prevented, and turn it into a positive outcome to help save other lives.

Some people have created events, programs, and organizations to bring awareness and prevent future related deaths.

Examples:
MADD - Mother's Against Drunk Driving
Mom's Demand Action
Rachel's Challenge

Focus on life, not the death when possible.

Draw and color a team jersey.

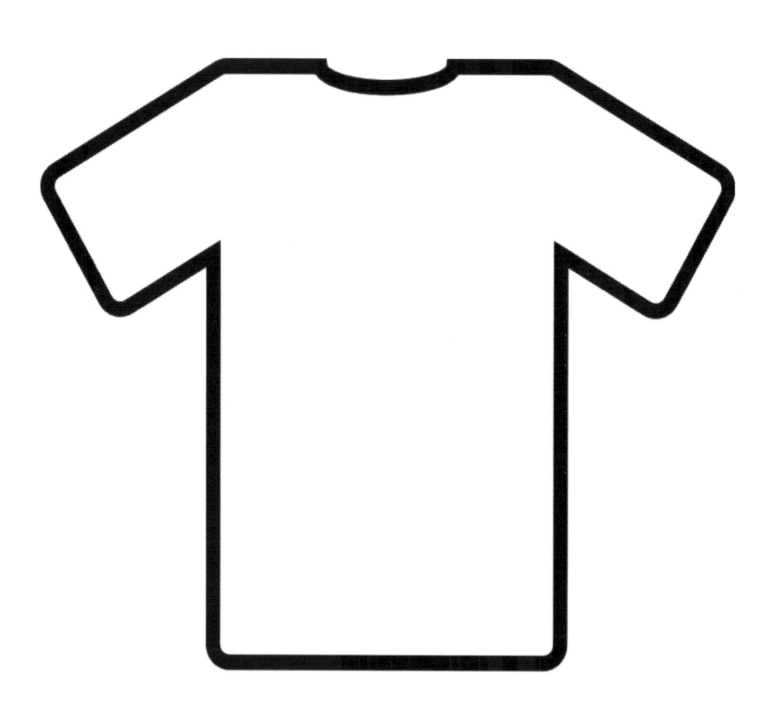

Every day, see who you can help,
so there will be a better tomorrow.

* Remember to give yourself lots of love and pamper yourself with things you love to do and surround yourself with people and pets that love and support you.

Sometimes just a caring smile and a hug makes a huge difference to a person that is experiencing grief or a loss of a loved one.

Discussion questions that kids may bring up with adults.

- What do you think happens to people when they die?

- Did you ever deal with the death of someone you loved? How did you get through it?

- Is it normal for me to sometimes think about my own death? Do you ever do the same thing?

- What would happen to me if you died?

- What are the different causes of death. (See next page)

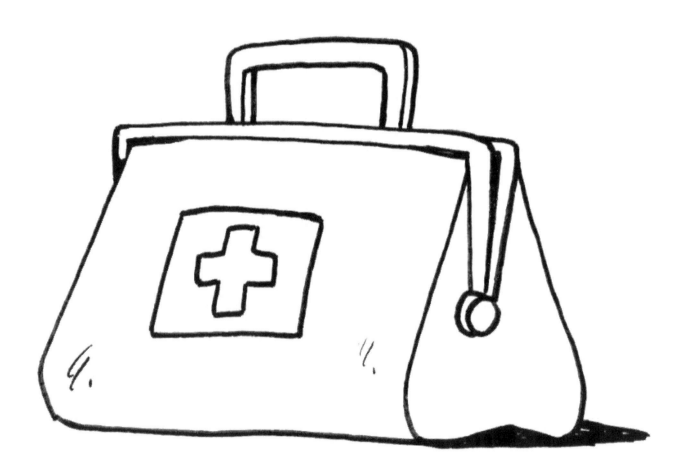

WHAT ARE THE DIFFERENT CAUSES OF DEATH?

There are several causes of death, listed below:

❑ **<u>Diseases</u>**

Examples: Cancer, Heart Disease, AIDS, Diabetes.

❑ **<u>Illnesses</u>**

Examples: Pneumonia, Polo, Flu, Infections.

❑ **<u>Accidents</u>**

<u>Examples</u>: Car Accidents, Chokings, Drowning's, Fires.

❑ **<u>Weather Related</u>**

<u>Examples</u>: Tornadoes, Hurricanes, & Earthquakes.

❑ **<u>Crime/Violence Related</u>**

<u>Examples</u>: Gun Shootings, Stabbings.

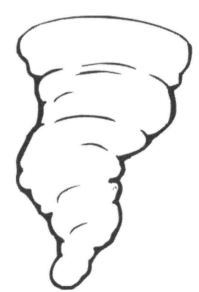

❑ **<u>War Related</u>**

<u>Examples</u>: Bombs, Guns, Weapons.

Questions Following a Death:

- What's going to happen at the funeral? Can I participate in the funeral? What if I don't feel like going at all?

- How can I find ways to let out these feelings I'm having? Can we come up with things to do together that might help both of us?

- If I think I need to talk to someone, like a therapist or a pastor from our place of worship, can you help me arrange that?

- Are there places where I can meet and talk to other kids who are going through the same thing?

What is a funeral?

A funeral is a ceremony marking a person's death, usually held at a church. A coffin holds the person's body, and is at the alter with a lot of flowers around the coffin to honor that person.

At most funerals many people will talk about the person's life, show pictures, and play music. After the funeral, the loved one is buried in the ground or cremated.

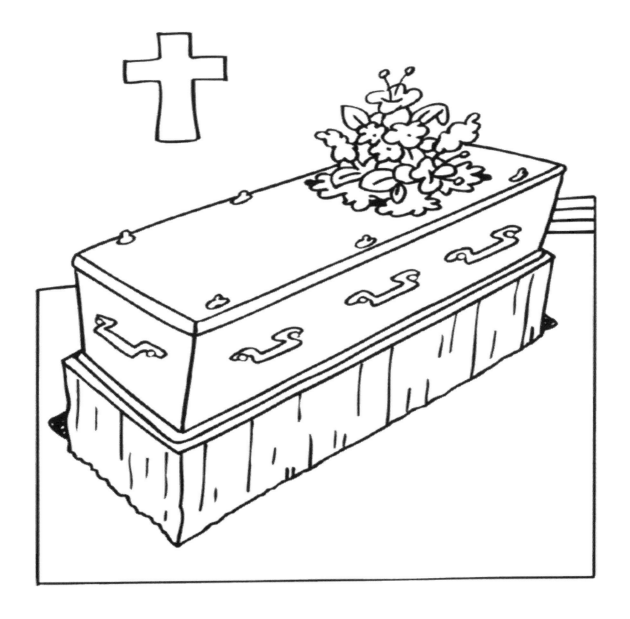

* A child who is frightened about attending a funeral should not be forced to go; however, some service or observance is recommended, such as lighting a candle, saying a prayer or visiting a grave site.

Made in the
USA
Columbia, SC